# Cute Duff

by Justin Musser
illustrated by Luanne Marten

Practice Decodable 85

Mc Graw Hill Education

Bothell, WA • Chicago, IL • Columbus, OH • New York, NY

**MHEonline.com**



Send all inquiries to:
McGraw-Hill Education
8787 Orion Place
Columbus, OH 43240-4027

ISBN: 978-0-02-145431-0
MHID: 0-02-145431-0

Printed in China.

8 9 10 11 12 DSS 27 26 25 24 23

The Dale family was big. There were six kids! The Dale house was filled with fun.

The Dales got a new, cute pup. They named him Duff. Five Dale kids played with Duff, fed Duff, and hugged Duff.

But Bobby Dale did not like the pup much. Bobby did not play with Duff or hug him.

Bobby was a music pupil. He played the bugle. Bobby hoped to be in a band.

When Bobby played, Duff ran to Bobby's room. Duff would try to make music like Bobby did. Duff made singing sounds.

The family liked Duff's cute music. Bobby did not! "Pups cannot sing with a music pupil," Bobby said.

Soon Bobby would not let Duff in his room. But Duff still sat on the hall rug and sang with Bobby's bugle.

When Bobby played, the five Dale kids took Duff to a huge park. Duff ran, jumped, and had fun.

One day, Duff ran too far. The kids could not find him. Did Duff run away? The five Dales ran home.

Mom and Dad led a hunt for Duff. "Duff! Duff!" the Dale family called and called.

Would the Dale family ever find cute, little Duff? How could they get him back? Mom knew how.

Bobby was playing his bugle. "We cannot find Duff in the huge park," said Mom.

Bobby looked sad. He really did like cute, little Duff. Like Mom, Bobby knew how to find the pup.

Bobby played in the park. Soon Duff was next to him. The Dales clapped as Bobby and Duff made music!